This Thing of Memory

The Impact and Commemoration of
the First World War in Poetry

by

David Hynes

with a Foreword by Phil Carradice

First Published in 2014
by GWL Publishing
an imprint of Great War Literature Publishing LLP

Produced in United Kingdom

ISBN 978-1-910603-01-7 Paperback Edition

GWL Publishing
Forum House
Sterling Road
Chichester PO19 7DN
www.gwlpublishing.co.uk

Born in Preston, Lancashire, David studied Modern History at St Andrews University where he first came to love poetry in general and war poetry in particular.

In 2004, David completed a Masters Degree in Journalism at Napier University, Edinburgh where he worked for various publications, from newspapers to magazines as well as writing online copy. He loved Edinburgh but his wanderlust exceeded all else and in 2008-2009 he travelled extensively throughout South and Central America where he learnt Spanish and taught English as a foreign language. It was here that David encountered Pablo Neruda's poetry and learnt about the works of Marquez, Vargas and Borges.

Once back in England, amidst great procrastination, David moved to Didsbury in Manchester in 2010, first for a girl, and then for a job.

He is currently self-employed, working as a freelance writer and supply teacher and even occasionally (and only for fun) as an actor.

Phil Carradice is a poet, novelist and historian. He has written over fifty books, his most recent novel being "Do Not Go Gentle," about the death of poet Dylan Thomas. He writes a weekly blog for BBC Wales History and presents the Radio Wales history programme "The Past Master."

DEDICATION

This collection is dedicated to my family, my parents especially, and to my friends. Their help and encouragement was essential and greatly appreciated.

Acknowledgements

This is my first poetry anthology and I owe my gratitude to certain persons. I would like to thank Wendy Lawrance, my publisher, for her efforts in getting this collection together. Her feedback was very helpful in revising these poems. Also, my thanks to David Beckler, a member of a writing group I attend in Manchester who told me about GWL publishing. Without him I wouldn't have met Wendy. My thanks, also, to Phil Carridice for his agreeing to write an foreword for this collection.

The *BBC* archives and *The Daily Telegraph's* features on the First World War were often helpful in finding the inspiration of what to write about. Also, David Stevenson's *1914-1918; The History of the First World War*, Max Hasting's *Catastrophe; Europe Goes to War 1914* and Max Arthur's *Forgotten Voices* were insightful sources of information.

CONTENTS

Foreword

It might be something of a generalisation but, for most of us, our view of the First World War – the Great War as it was universally known until our government decreed otherwise after the second great bloodletting of the twentieth century – has been shaped and formed by the poets who wrote so movingly about the conflict and their involvement in it.

Sassoon, Owen, Rosenberg, Gurney and the rest have left us with an enduring and graphic vision of the war – perhaps a little one-sided but, then, having experienced the events of 1914-18 in the way that they did, it is hardly surprising.

When we think of the classic First World War concepts – lions led by donkeys, the mud and squalor of the trenches, incessant frontal attacks on fixed defensive positions, men walking to their death in No Man's Land – it is their version of the war that controls our thinking, their images that impinge themselves into our brains.

The words of the war poets have influenced novelists, playwrights, film makers and historians of many nationalities and generations. It has been like that since Sassoon first published his satirical volume, *Counter Attack and Other Poems*, in the last year of the war.

For poets to have such a profound effect on the sensibilities of so many succeeding generations, is a testament both to the skill of the writers and to the experiences they shared. The fact that poetry has the ability to conjure and control such emotions is what makes it such a powerful medium, one that writers still use in an attempt to – explain is the wrong word – to achieve some degree of understanding of, and empathy with, what went on in those four terrible years.

David Hynes was not there in the trenches or at Jutland, he did not endure the rats and the gas and the barbed wire – he was too young; he was not even born - but in this remarkable collection he has used that very distance to create objectivity. That doesn't make the poems any less profound or telling. If anything, it has made the collection even more powerful

I think it was Philip Larkin who said that if Gerard Manley Hopkins had been a survivor from the "Deutschland" his poem about the shipwreck would have been much less effective. Sound advice and words that Larkin himself used when writing "1914," his own haunting comment on the war.

It is the same with David Hynes and "This Thing of Memory". Writing at a distance only gives the words and his view of the events added power. Wilfred Owen might have said that the poetry was in the pity; here the pity and the need to remember are clearly redolent in the poetry. There is compassion but it is controlled – partly by distance, partly by the writer's skill – and that makes it far more than a simple knee jerk reaction to catastrophe.

Hynes has an intuitive sense of history. He uses this knowledge to power the poems but at no time does it ever intrude on the instinctive desire to be a poet. He has a wide range of style and form. Everything from free verse to traditional structures is to be found here in a collection that is profound, sure of itself and, at times, deeply ironic. His often repeated line from the poem "Daddy" is just one example. The phrase, "What did you do in the great commemoration daddy?" stays with you long after the poem has been put down.

That irony does not damage the compassion, however, compassion that runs through the poems like lifeblood. And yet that crucial emotion is not cloying or sentimental. These words, these images, are hard-hitting and profound and have a degree of realism that is reminiscent of the war poets themselves. As Hynes says:-

In Auschwitz, which came later
And eviller, it's true,
You can still smell the evil.
But here in Flanders, too,
A perfume still holds out.

That's what makes a poet: the ability to pick up on tiny moments or ideas. The smell of evil may well be used by many to describe the remains of Auschwitz but how many would ever contemplate joining the word "perfume" with the filth of Flanders in the Great War?

"This Thing of Memory" is a significant achievement, one that will out-last the centenary commemorations. And that's how it should be. These are poems of skill and lasting significance – only time will tell how lasting they will be. However, if there is any justice in the world, this collection and this poet will be remembered for a very long time indeed.

Phil Carradice, 2014

Introduction

The centenary of the First World War almost took us by surprise. We were all busy doing things. We had places to be. We were in a rush. We were online, filtering our swamps of information for what was most relevant, most pressing.

It felt faintly preposterous that something like a world war would have much relevance to us. A hundred years is a long time and we are too distant from it, too removed from the madness of going to fight, en masse, in another country, unsure of our return.

And what were we supposed to do? Think about the war? Watch television programmes about it? Listen to radio plays about the Western Front? What on earth was this centenary meant to evoke? Anything? Should it mean anything to us?'

For some it meant very little, except as an over-hyped news item often attached to the end of broadcasts. For others it meant a little more. Based on an obligation of memory and guilt, for them the centenary was like a musty silence; its commemoration was to be observed in a state of mild contemplation.

But to a smaller demographic, and I include myself in this, it meant nothing short of an adventure. An attempt to study, learn and relive something that felt both close and distant, something that wavered in the consciousness as an essential, almost spiritual investigation with the simultaneous paranoia of its irrelevance and futility. In simple terms, the centenary asked me a direct question. It asked, 'What does this mean to you?'

'A lot,' I said, content this was a good answer. Then it, or I, asked a second, much harder question. 'Why?'

This question, above all, spurred me into doing a little – then a lot – of research into the Great War. The more I dug, the more I found. Some things struck me as being particularly relevant. In my own lifetime there was been a generational schism between pre- and post-internet and pre- and post- 9/11 worlds. The Great War (aptly named) was its own schism. The world faced a cliff in 1914 and by 1918 it had fallen off it. Driven off it, some would argue.

So, too, the scope of the war struck me as being immense. The depth, range and intensity of the fighting, the capacity for war to affect life at all levels – civilian and military, belligerent and neutral – and the extent of global mobilisation to conduct the war were all incredible to me. So, too, was the scope for innovation within the war itself. Tanks, planes, submarines; all the product of innovative reactions in the pursuit of finding better ways to kill each other.

Also refreshing was finding out how the stain of the war's reputation as being a futile, cruel conflict was not borne out by the people fighting it at the time. Fresh perspectives and reappraisals of the war continue to divide historians and the common memory of the war requires these reappraisals. We think about something in the terms of what we think we know about it and we don't know what we don't yet know.

But the strangest thing of all which I found in my research was how totally human the people involved were. Sometimes we think of the past in too grandiose terms. We think that what we sculpt marble for, what we wear poppies for, what we stay in silence for, is exalted. It belongs to the exotic and distant past.

This is not the case. It is neither accurate nor helpful to unduly exalt something in terms of our being able to empathize with it. Wars are no different.

We can study what happens to a people when caught up in a war, when the world steers right over a cliff. We can ask counterfactuals and endless whatifs – whatshoulds might be the better term – but after a while we must accept what happened did indeed happen for its own beguiling reasons; usually because it was the result of people acting like people. Wars, for all their machinery and strategies and sense of distance, have people at their heart. People facing dilemmas and making choices and not knowing what the consequences will be always occupy the very centre of a war's drama.

And when we, one hundred years on, look around us and see the cosmic illogicality of our own situation, of the traumatic suffering of the poor, the ludicrous behaviour of the rich, the unknowability of our place in the world – from our daily routine to the vitriol and peace that exists between nations – we can only really say at the end of it all that we are people acting like people do.

It doesn't take much research, then to come to the dumbstruck and fantastic conclusion that a hundred years is not so long at all.

And if you're not going to study it now, if you don't take an interest in it on its anniversary – its great, big, fat 100th birthday – will you ever? The next big thing, let's face it, is the two hundred years mark and, cynical as I am, I don't hold out too much hope our offspring will be digging ditches in their backyard on August 4th 2114 to investigate the vicariousness of trench-life.

Do your digging now. The First World War is well worth the revisit and you will find glittering revelations in the soil that sparkle with relevance and interest.

Lest we forget.

David Hynes, 2014

This Thing of Memory

If I am thirty years and this thing of trenches and
    shell and shellshock and flu and dirt
And desperation is a hundred, I can conceive it – its
    conception is not blurred. It's me;
Three and a third.

This thing of a cenotaph is not so far as all that. You
    see, I had it as ancient. Those dark,
Alien landscapes now with their crosses and their
    plaques. Had them as just too long
Ago to remember anything back.

But hold up, it's my dad times one point four, or
    granddad, if he weren't gone the way
Of the big snore, be granddad one point two to get
    there – now that is close – that's
Practically anew.

And for my offspring, how my dad would like to
    know when the white dresses and the
Foetus will grow, will it be them times ten, this
    ancient thing? As recent as a wren.

Famous

CS Lewis found his wardrobe in the mud fields of
   escapism.
Tolkien his wizards in his trench fever dreams and
   Milne
Found Winnie the Pooh amongst the wider sadism
   and screams.

Moore found his sculptures amidst the gas attacks of
   Cambrai –
Hubble his telescope, e.e. cummings his style, Brecht
   his theatre, Hitler
His bile.

Churchill his redemption in his mad forays into No-
   Mans-Land;
De Gaulle his resistance, Göring his propaganda,
   and Pope John
XXIII pandered to God's great hand. –

And did Bogart find his cigars? Holst his planets;
    particularly Mars.
Basil Rathbone his deduction. Chevalier his, well, his
    je ne sais quoi,
And did Chandler, dozing with a Browning
    machine-gun at his feet,
Wink his worried and weary Big Sleep

And did Hemingway glimpse his Farewell to Arms
Driving his ambulance in stark alarm? Did Mussolini
Tailor his black shirts here, Priestley answer to his
    Inspectors
Calling? And an unravelling Ravel find his bloodied
    Bolero
Amongst the bloodied falling?

And when we see the roll call of famous soldiers –
Not to belittle the common register one bit – can we
Conclude anything about war's impact on the
    would-be-
Just-you-and-me's and the would-go-on-to-be-that's?

Not really.

Hear It?

Hear the sounds of London fall into a zero
Hear the gossip wait for its phlegm to reload
Hear the papers nudge each other at this unexpected
   holiday
Hear the traffic lights place their hands above their
   mouths
And cough a quick amber shy.

Hear the urban fox's scampered manumission
Hear the bread grenades giving pigeon permission
Hear the leather loafers salute in silence with those
   asleep
Under the holes-in-the-wall whilst the hole-in-the-
   noise of the city
Creeps its silence and even the birds and the dogs
   stay quiet
At this human tremor and all the statues squint at
   this
Pantomime reversal in the London riot.

Hear that. Silence, one minute last
Hear the roar of soldiers
Marching through the past
Hear a century stop, a century's journey
A citizen's Judge and Jury – an Allied attorney.

Hear the trenches ferret over the fences
And survey the weeds of a century's rot.
Hear those trees, whose branches shush the
Squirrels and hear the swans behave a minute of
    their
Queen's best and even push noisy mallards aside and
Smother them with beakfuls of admonishment.
Beakfuls of the secular shush water.

And the people drink it too
All of Oxford Street as silent as an unbuilt zoo
Its monkeys know something is about
And the worst thing to do would be to idly shout.

The minute feels longer, fatter – more full
A Vigil, A Rite, a Milestone, a profundity-pull
Hear what it is and hear what it suggests
And all the poppies, and all the rest.

What Did The Birds Think?

On their haunting, awesome migration did they stop
   – yes in mid-air,
Stop like a cat had sprung from some high-hovering
   lair and gazed down upon
The moving things and free fall in disarray –
And ask, 'What is that they have there?
And what are they doing now, these insatiables?'

And were they looking at the tanks or the planes that
   spread over
France at Champagne or was it gliding over the Med
   for some long-haul,
Winter-fled when they saw the U-Boats slither out on
   the surface like smiling
Crocodiles until they submerged,
'See you in a hellish while, you lucky out-of-reach
   birds.'

And as they Africa reached and shook their beaks at
    men
And their strange flights of fancy, did they see the
    lowly beasts
Of the Serengeti, and decide that man's ways are
    more foul?

Ultimately, they will never land too long, never stay
    too long on land,
And never, they affirm, evolve too much. For look at
    the ostrich in flight
And those mammals below of a deep, dark night.

France, 12/11/1918

A pays ne pas;
Brisé, détruit, ruiné, words like that.
Cities now vineyards of debris and rubble,
Villages swept away in cloves of trouble.
France on its knees, its towns without églises,
Brittle villages in a sledgehammer's fury.
A country's childhood of burned out écoles,
The countryside craterized, the bells
Too broke to toll.

The Allied Prayer

Had Germany won, as Germany done,
In peace as it had in war,
And give us these terms not
As neo-Christians but as
Mad dogs, given in to temptation,
As in pillage, as in war.
For the Kaiser would be
The United Kingdom, the power
And the glory,
For to the victor goes the spoils,
The winner writes the story.

Courage, Also

That courage can be twofold, a yes and a no, that courage
can take many forms, from the Duel to the no-show.

That callings can be wild and causes can be tame; one man's
green light is another man's Shame.

Some brave things risk disgrace.

Jeered in egg-lobbed ridicule, jailed, disenfranchised, their
drinks never clinked, their Birthdays
Never cheered – whole families torn between brothers and
sisters of volunteers and
Resisters.

A tornado of primal emotions unleashed as of the old
schoolyard fights. The country in a State of ecstasy about
the goodness of war – they were all so certain, they were all
so sure.

And with war's end and audits horrific commence in a new
light studied those men who said 'No'.
And Resisters resisting the desire to say 'I told you so.'

A U-Boat and a Blue Whale Meet at Last, Circa 1915

Echoes rebound, echo again amongst the lost and found.
Swish with their fins in full finesse and then, from this
Swishing and finning and flapping of sorts, comes another
Double-double. Deadlock; mirror-impasse runs aground.

And they part, these two giants of submariners lore,
These two contests of Latin-Saxons and nature-man law.
These two from God and Atheism who swim with great
    grace
These two – one chaser; one chaste.

We Won And We Celebrate It

The biggest secret which all Europe knows. That the
  beers would
Be brimming, the haus full of singing no matter
  what the cost,
The reason for low-key German parties is that they
  bloody lost.

The British War Cemetery in Gaza

Almost Andalusian the way they have a certain
   harmony,
Muslims, Jews and Christians all asleep and in good
   keep
With only clashes outside the greensward to stir
   them
From their not-botheredness.

And those grave-trodden noises, do they make them
Weep, or is that the water from above for those well-
Kept tombs of sufficient good rain to varnish the
   rust –
War with stars and crosses and Ottomans who fell in
Full roar?

This sanctuary, sweetened by jacaranda trees,
Would belie the greater eternity; is it in here,
Where the best of the living preserve themselves,
Is it here the dignity of man's fate lies, sleeping by
The sides of those who took up and then
Threw down similar prides?

Or is outside the gates the true escape,
Where beliefs clash and clash,
Where those well-kept sprinkled lawns are dying
To know the score, of who's fighting who and
   whether
In play, romp, scratch or claw.

I think not.

The Gaza War Cemetery, island amidst the torrent,
Place of such piety it invites clichés with or without
Cliché warrants. 'An idyll' it hear the chatters above
Say ten gazalillion times, 'a message to the fighters
   outside'
They've heard more than water was had without
   wine.
And they sleep at it all.

Jews, Christians and Muslims, sleep it all off in the
Well-kept Gaza War Cemetery.

Harlem Hellfighters

In newsreel black and white we watch the fighting
   now
And we see those mud faces and we see the ancient
   row.
Of shades and shapes of Gods and apes. Of ideas
   and their rashes.
Of men and of mice; of the mitre and nitre in all
   belief's clashes.

And in this almost-stick-figure valour of the
   newsreel's mad dance
These shapes move-in enfilade or belly-down with
   courage-gut or
Sand-bagging or lugging something heavy around.
   Yet there is one final
Shade, an-almost fade, in the madness of wartime-
   furrowed France;

The men-wronged, the men whom the French declaimed as
Those stalwart Men of Bronze – the 369th, the American
Braves, heavier-loaded men in this life God made, but who
Took it the lighter and made it the brighter; the men whom the

Germans christened as the Harlem Hellfighters. A spice of
Sizzle, of life in the gristle and they tickled their Jazz amongst
The mud as the Gods of War swung and sweetened French
Grime with their syrup play – a story so not-known enough and

That sticky sugar sparked by James Reese Europe, the boogie-man
With the surname of the trenches but who sprang from lands in-
Dentured, cotton-plucking kingdoms rotten where men still saw
Newsreel black and white of moonshine and summer nights and

In legacy we know their time was not quite there and
how
Sometimes ideas break free and other times they
repair.
And your Victory Parade the sprightliest New York
had
Ever seen – and then the sunset Red Summer of
1919.

The Ditch

Today I've dug a ditch.
Taken the day off work.
My interest hitched,
A suspicion lurked;

I lie here,
The neighbours watch.
Not to relieve me
But to call the cops.

I lie in this grease,
And this offensive dirt.
Resigned to attrition
But on the alert.

This corset of mud
Has my courage stanched.
Has me squirming like a mole –
Pretending it's France.

And this sullied claustrophobia,
Which remembers my goal,
Has me peeping out the turrets
Of my back lawn's knolls.

And the question's outbreak,
Incubated for the morning's duration,
Gives my subterranean pilgrimage
A warning's citation;

How do men lie in a trench for so long,
The only relief the sound of a bomb?
How did they do it? I don't think I could.
How did they stay so long in the mud?

The question itched
I scratch my suburbia
All neighbour-waving and
Wiping dirty knees.

And to think,
The poor bastards, still-to-come –
The wretched Senor's sneeze.

Somme 1

Prairie dogs. Squirrels. Peeping rodents. Airborne meals.
From the sperm in the womb which won the rabid race
And became a me or a you, here's a tomb-reversal, and a
Troubling about-face.
We are stuck, slow and slothful, sluggish as glue.
We move, but do not make haste.

Do not swim for your life. Plod to your death.
Do not return fire, laden yourself with
Cumbersomes and awkwards –
For Death hates a trier.

We, the Volunteers, on our first day at the office,
Trundle around to view the submarine in the field
With its open hatch of lemmings braving the open-keeled.
We watch them disappear these life-triers, we Orpheusonians
With our thirty kilogram lyres know we shouldn't have
    looked –
Head onwards for the blasted, barbed wires.

We slide back, some of us, back to the submarine
Should-be-sealed, which in fact is an open-coffin.
A nice open-coffin in the mud and we do slide back
Amongst the squelching and the thuds. We slide back, some
Of us, because we prefer the coffin to death.

But others have made it, all the way
To the subs' gun turrets which are meant
To be dead. They have revived themselves, however,
For easy pickings like this require a gamesmanship
Alongside the banquet's bread.

Prairie Dogs. Squirrels. Hatchling turtles. Crab-crunched,
About to die scrubbed on the sand or plucked by the groping
Heron birds' heady high command.

Unable, I think, to swim even if we
Make water, though we know we can't stay on land.
It's the lesser of two awfullers.

But the froth and spume of wave
Was a hard blow to take. For the barbed wire is more barbed
And Medusa angry we hath made. 'Shell me all day long,'
She shrieks. 'Though you know you cannot pass.
I've survived my own reflection,' cried the Anglo-Saxon lass.

The Lost Villages

'Grande Rue' the little blue sign goes in long-deserted
  Bezonvaux
'Was once the main little strip' it still blabbers to the
  surrounding trees,
'Where you would find a boucherie, a boulangerie and a
  colourful little épicerie,'
It sighs and half dies to see its breath faint on the breeze,
  mocked by those playful
And quaint little forest fairies.

The same for Fleury-devant-Douaumont, away again in
  silent détente.
And Ornes, long now in convalesce.
Or Haumont-prés-Samogneux – the creaks of the barks now
  the only stir.
And in Cumiéres le Mort Homme all that's left is unexploded
  bombs.

The Lost Villages, where the haunted voices of lost sons
  disappear into glum forests
Nurtured wild. Forests so dense, human memory is its only
  sun. Forests encouraged
To drink up Verdun.

The War to End All Wars

Perhaps it felt like that before. That from this war or that war
Surely we or they would never bother with such a thing
    again.
Then, when this one, The Great War, not the damned First
    World War
But The Great War, came along, it was different. It was so
    different
It must have been a high-point to which no one would ever
    ascale again.
It made sense, give it titular closure for such a thing would
    never twice foment.

Who would use the aircraft except to ferry folk from
    Bournemouth to the USA
Or from the USA to Stoke? Who would deploy the tanks?
    Lest it was some prank,
Carting the married couple on a flower-drenched landship,
    or else bushwacking
Through a field on some old pals nostalgia trip?

Who could ever rape the countryside like this? And why?
    What possible motive?
Who would sit in a ditch again or bayonet a man's face?
    Certainly not the Russians.
For they are so keen for people to refute the orders of their
    government and army
They are revolting. This civil war of theirs shows you how
    strong the feeling is.
The Russians won't do this again, I think – whether red,
    white or pink.

And not the Germans either. Versailles will be their decider.
    Besides, they just won't.
Firstly we won't let them and secondly you can tell. They are
    like us.
They want nothing of it. It is Teutonic-ally-thus.

Nor the French. You think they would host such a thing
    twice? They'd permit this mess
Again? Don't you think they have wine to drink, girls to kiss,
    snails to Maintain?
And for that matter, not the Belgians. They've had their spell
    of non-neutrality and
Side-picking for them is often seldom.

And not us. The Great War Great Britoners. The boys from
    God's Green Country;
The boys of Mr Kitchener. We wouldn't dream. In fact, so
    we figure, the next
Archduke to cop it gets an OBE – so too the man who pulls
    the trigger. No, we assure
You we've had enough, thank you. Anyone wants to rise up
    again from the phoenix of
These sacred ashes, they would be mad, we will not get
    involved, it would take
Something utterly disastrous for the War to End All Wars to
    not be the all-told.

The Stench of Youth

In Auschwitz, which came later
And eviller, it's true,
You can still smell the evil.
But here in Flanders, too,
A perfume still holds out.

Is it evil, this thing in the nose and the mind?
No. It's sad.
It's sadness not evil.
Though people were bunched together in a
Small dirty place to work and die just the same,
There is a knowingness at Auschwitz
Which Flanders cannot claim.

For the smell of sadness is virile
And here's the hidden truth,
It's the smell of innocence turned sour
Which rates this evil lour.
It is the smell of innocence at a loss;
Inhale it; cry, even – but don't be cross.

And like a Virgin cemetery
Bedecked with letters hoped-for
The smell here is of captured roses
A smell of a stolen cure.
It's the smell of experimentation
Though not the biological kind
It is a stench of modernisation
Old ghosts bravely declined.

Out here the scent of sadness
Is the most exalted redolence on Earth.
Not evil, the fields exhale to those memorial-
Breathers who nod at its eczema of scarred
Crosses and its pockmarks of cough.
Not evil. Just sad.

New Boss

And catapulted into the war, first by rustlings of a
    democratic credo,
Then concretely by the whizz of a torpedo –
And then by telegram eyesoar –

The Americans sprinted, cannonball and brimstone,
And Yee-haws with money loans into the gold medal
    spot –
Economy booming, jazz hands grooving –

Oh and the black cars they drove and
Oh the sheer length of their roads.
They had such space – not on the map and
Not to everyone's taste –
And they had, above all, Rudolph Valentino.

The Tunnellers

Half-blind with half a candle's lick, praying the 'setts' would
   hold,
Thankful for no quicksand slick
And thankful more for the canary to dandle,
Shooting glances at the mice, listening to the birdsong's
   demise
On which is perched your life – all this,
In the deep, dark, dastardly gloom.
And just as the war couldn't get any deeper- a tremor, a U-
   bahn mole,
Coming your way; and there isn't any room.

With picks and knives and shovels and knuckles
You swipe in the darkness, half-forgotten, glad to know
Hell won't be near as shabby.
You wrestle and win, stabbing them grim,
And continue on as before with
Kicker, Bagger and Trammer, trolleying out the dirt and
Laying your mines – waiting for the earth to list and lurch.

And chirping in high silence at this quick victory,
You funnel further, and a leaking of blood
Stalks through the tunnel and paints your boots.
And your still-alive canary pet hears rumours of
More Germans about. So you wink at your canary
And Lay your camouflets.
Wide-eared and wary; worried of their own scouts.

Above ground, worlds away, the infantry sees the
Enemy camp implode and nod in thanks at the work
Of these now-remembered, now-glimpsed men-moles.
And below, you nod your head too, down in this malevolent
Underworld.

You nod at war's careful avalanches.

As this time it was German tunnellers who lost –
      brave men all.
It was they who suffocated. They who were tossed
In the wroth mud sea. Their Skeletons in every repose of
      horror,
Half-forgotten, like the world's past,
Closer to the earth's core than before, further, perhaps, from
      the stars.
Underground. Seeping. Unexhumed. Never found.

The Explosion at Messines

They heard it first in Dover, and the chalk phewed
  with dust,
Its spray-sheath settling like a linen-mail of
  whitened, writhened crust –
And the chalk did strive to protect itself from the
  bellow of the bang –
And it was the chalk that heard first, the bell which
  mankind rang.

Next to go deaf with knowledge of what we can do
  and what we might –
In some deeper and darker despair, in some
  dastardly din-dead night
Was a listening part of quietude, a south-easterly
  heard-hood which sensed
The heavens being prised apart by an irregular
  future tensed.

Then came an aspect of London, luscious really with
    euphonious views,
A des-res suburb of looters and suitors, all clattered,
    cloying and bruised.
Where waiters blew raspberries at children and
    wooed at the winking mothers,
Where all the gathered turned to Ben – 'was this
    some even bigger brother?'

And even wider the roundel goes for those who
    heard it slower,
Those who heard trace-later the grumblings of this
    human Krakatoa;
And they guessed at what had blown up. A body?
    Ten bodies? Twenty?
And they guessed at what it meant. This loudness,
    this incendiary energy.

Had a country blown up, perhaps?
For the noise was as big as France Is French.
Or, worse yet, a century?
Or was it just a body after all?
The simple sleeping feet of a single misguided sentry.

It Wasn't So Bad

And it was all horrors this and horrors that? We didn't
Joke and smoke and slap the backs of those who shared our
    midden.
No, it wasn't five star. It's not cinq etoile, being a pal.
But apart from Bournemouth, that was our only holiday thus
    far,
And for all its evil, the four thousand calories a day
Somewhat mellowed the upheaval.
No it wasn't good, of course. And Great is really stretching it.
But nor was it filled with this all-profound rapport.
It was life.
It was duty.
It was something you got on with – be it ugly, be it beauty.
World War Two, the good one? World War One, the futile?

Gas and all that, hellish, brutal, innocences lost.
It was war. We were men. Such is the eternity of life
The always now and the always then.
Don't let Owen and Sassoon deceive you.
There are other voices long, long worth their due.
It was a strange old time alright, but don't just listen to those
    two.

Daddy

What did you do in the great commemoration
   daddy,
What did you do in its centenary?

Were you inspired by your couch,
Inspired as you profoundly slouched
And nodded at the memorial's flickering pictures;
'That's right,' you exclaim.
'That's right. This is what it means to be British.
'This is what it means to honour their fight.'

Or did you do something extra?

Something a bit harder.

Did you start to festoon the village memorial
In simple little flowers?
Did you salute it, at quiet, ungodly hours?

And did you organise some feat?
Some little tribute march in our little
Sleepy street?

What did you do in the Great Centenary, Daddy?
Did you just slouch,
Or did you remember with your feet?

For As Long As We Can

Age shall not weary them.
Yes it will.
But this fate is inevitable
Like the death on the sill
Of the sun-starved stem.

What tears for the English Civil War
Or our Hundred with the French?
What long bows for Agincourt,
And for Yorktown, what laments?

2014 asks us for mark of memory
With its splintered-beset bench;
Yet how deluged was the Ekumeku Movement,
And so – how drenched will be the trench?

A few choice words we'll muster
Perhaps in 2114,
When a double-century seen
Will hit for six the Good Men cluster
Of those Great War Tragedians

Though cricket and Englishness
May long be tattle
We may preserve, at least,
The semantics of their battle

Roundheads. Cavaliers. Spion Kop.
Over the top.
Big Bertha. Trenches, maybe. Or Gas.
Maybe not.

And a hundred from now if only desert and war
Terrorism, extremism and yearly weather storms
Be the semantic relics of present zealots
We, the present-future centenarians keep aglow
The futile law;
That every age is equal
With equal sized despair.

That all the prequels and all the sequels
And the forget leaks can't repair
And the to-comes and already-rans.
We will remember then
Beyond a century's span.
Or at least, we promise them,
For as long as we can
For as long as we can.

Somme 2

Twenty-thousand dead in twenty-four hours.
The day which still sticks in our throats.
The nadir battle, the infamous, blood-dripping
Mammoth in the room of Britain upon which we
Lack a scour.

The most fatalities in a chunk of British time.
The blood hands in a startling rush.
And this to break the deadlock,
This to change the phase of war;
This the overstated 'Big Push'.

Somme 3

A day when Fish and Chips where ruined
By the ketchup of our organs,
And every Toad-in-its-Hole was ravaged
By a grisly, gory Gorgon.
And dover-souls simply fried in their own
Oil-wounds.

A day of British morning strolls
In sober disarray.
A day of derring-do, well-observed,
In the bumbling, British way.

Well-observed, well-kept, well-met,
In silent funeral carol.
A day the Saxons left the house,
Wet their Saxon mouths
And slaughtered fat fish in a flimsy,
Thinning barrel.

1 July 1916. Bad day; bad battle –
The worst we've ever had.

But from this cock-up we enrolled
And learnt our living heads.
We washed the old supper down and
Earned our living bread;

We said never again, and never
Since has day nor battle been half as wretched,
Half as sad.

The Didsbury Village War Memorial

Just opposite Tesco as it goes
And right next to one of the best beer shops in
    Manchester –
Carringtons – stocks everything, wheat beers,
    microbreweries from the States,
French wines (expensive), you name it; they have it.
Close to the library and close to Aldi and near a little
    coffee shop which often plays Vivaldi –
To which those commuters on the long road to
    Stockport say, 'hear that, we are in Didsbúry'

Almost a kind of frontispiece, nice little memorial it
    is, especially when the sun's out
And this urbane suburb comes alive with chequered
    shorts and tight tops and tight jeans
And colour and lace and all the beer gardens which
    surround it are packed –
Carringtons does a trade on warm days, and cheaper
    Aldi goes berserk on a hot day, and
Didsbury Village, being pretty affluent, is okay on a
    rainy day too.

But the statue, the memorial, the inscription, its
   tutorial, stays the same, whatever the weather,
   regardless of passing lace or leather or
   supermarket changes or beer connoisseur's Savvy
   exchanges. The inscription reads:

'DIDSBURY WAR MEMORIAL
1914-1919
TO THE MEMORY OF THE SACRED DEAD OF
THIS VILLAGE. WHO HAVING LEFT ALL
THAT WAS DEAR TO THEM, ENDURED
HARDSHIPS, FACED DANGERS, AND FINALLY
PAID THE SUPREME SACRIFICE IN DEFENCE
OF KING AND COUNTRY
"LET THEIR NAMES BE EVER REMEMBERED
WITH GRATITUDE.'

And then, as though in need of some simple
   valediction,

'MAY THEIR SOULS REST IN PEACE.'

The Cathedral at Reims

Too tall for its own good. So tall it touched God.
Whoever beheld it saw man's genius and whoever
Held it held the key to the city of Reims, watching
Bad men's revenge on much better men's dreams,
All in gross combat with God's great charter;
    whoever
Held it burned in the vaults of Cathedral Martyr.

The cathedral of coronation. The cathedral of
    kings.
The place where Joan of Arc knelt and clasped.
Its bedazzling rose window, its buttresses which
    reached
Rapturous for God's great grasp – stormed and
    shelled,
Crumbled they fell, like pagan cutlasses raining
    down from a
Squall-sieged mast.

And the priests waved their flags and the
Congregation in their rags broiled and fell amongst
Man's genius. Its transepts broken, its naves razed,
    the pews
Once-oaken crashed as the shells continued to fall.
    And the alter
Paid its sacrifice, imploding like a marble lamb in its
    shatter-cracked
Last rites.

And the Smiling Angel. The Smile of Reimes,
Whose head snapped off from falling beams
As the German's shelling frowned on and on.
As the lead dripped the gargoyles were ripped off
Their perch, for this, man's far-worse sermon.
But the smile returned.

The fabled Smile of Reimes restored. Still now,
    gleaming
Across all of France. Glistening, sparkling in its
    smile-shine.
And, in this sparkling spire world, testament to Man
    and
God and Time, The Smiling Angel is perched next
    to St Nicaise;
Whom the Bible tells us was martyred by being
    beheaded in the
Siege of Acre in Palestine.

Armenian Genocide/Lest We Forget

The truth can be washed away in tumble-spun eons.
A dot or a speck or a people can be erased.
If we don't remember, we'll likely forget.

Dirt can be forever washed away in silent-shushed
  paeans.
Do you remember what Hitler said?
'Who speaks today of the annihilation of the
  Armenians?'

Mud Cemetery

From a field came a coffin and in
This coffin went flesh and courage.
Most of my friend went in the coffin.
A coffin so tight-fitting he was squeezed,
Not through some parsimony of wood
But through the sheer excess of this endless mud.
Only his left leg escaped the shellburst
And its deadly, careless thud.

For his long left leg I do now keep,
In this trench, for my safeweep
Here is the long left leg of my friend
Which escaped, free-limb, Mud cemetery.

British at Caporetto

They came from Flanders; mudswamps, madness
    and glanders
Through the weather of Europe, til they met their
    new skyrise
Homes; the Alps, with its pinewoods ablaze and its
    snowy talc
Bubbling into a dreadful foam.
And did they know, these Brits who died alongside
    Italian friends –
Bombarded by Austrians to meet the highest of ends
    – they would
Become the first troops to cross pre-war boundaries
    into enemy territory?

The Bible War

And they pushed through lands made biblical
By names and men and faith. And they
    captured
Jerusalem; hallowed, humbled; in haste.

So Allenby, daring not to ride, not to foment
Any triumphalist scold, strides, unlike Jesus,
Through the sacred Jaffa Gate.

And the church bells in London and Rome
Chimed their holy noise when they heard the
Holy City had foot-fallen to Allenby and his
    boys.

Whose-Man's-Land

When we're done and Europe whoops
With the screams of tired peace
Will All Man's Land be No Man's Land
And All Men's Hands can Meet
Or is No Man's Land the euphemism
For which we dare not speak
You can put your trenches here boys
But up there is where we'll meet.

Chinese Labour Corps

Lured by mercenary missionaries in
The greatest outsourcing of Western
Jobs since fronts and ends began, all
Of them from far away and all of them
Silent. Near as distant as Japan.

Conveyed in giant hush-hush transits,
Their routes colossal. Swept across the
Pacific, quarantined in Canada. Examined;
Asked to sign off in any old hieroglyphic, and
Then shipped Atlantic-bound to arrive at a depot
Of dirt and gruel, as conspicuous as Confucius
And twice confused; as honorific as rookie
Pandas in some old grisly den. Still very much
Hush-hush, gung-ho and good-zen

Or tougher yet the war-migration went, via the
Suez and the Med. Onto Marseilles' anthem of
Blue, white and infinite red. U-boat targeted,
Land-loaded with spade and shovel and told
To dig, dig, dig monsieur orient, dig for me
For you are all now the diggers of the CLC!

And from that untapped labour that was tapped and
Tapped again, some Chinese men stayed in the
    Grande
Pays, with the blue and white the porcelain sky, the
    real France,
The opiate peace would claim,
And the stayers dug and drilled even faster to form
    the vivid
China-towns of Paris' sprinkled Diaspora.

They still have their baguettes and they still have
    their regrets and
Perhaps, they see, even today, when they look about
    them
That people can be displaced, head-hunted, desired,
    undesired
Chased, yearned and spurned and how some mad
    dogs run free
Whilst others sadly burn.

How Close We Were To Losing

Had the Lusitania stayed afloat,
Had French mutineers continued to choke.
Had the Final Offensive offended more,
Had the convoys taken longer to shore.

Had the Angel of Mons got a bit fruity,
Had Zimmerman not paid his stamp duty.
Had the Russians pulled out that bit sooner,
Had the naval blockade leaked some schooners.

Well, counterfactuals mean nothing to us,
Had it been too dry for Noah's flood,
Had the big bang not happened,
Had the Duke or JFK not met their assassin.
Still, when history is brimming with genius and
    blunder
Sometimes you must stop. Stop and wonder.

Battlefield Walk

Huddled, shoulder-to-shoulder, mindful of the
　　puddles
The penguins straggle and stumble,
Blood drizzling on their tuxedos –
Stiff upper beaks their magnificent credo.

But even the most stoical, the most
Fantastically heroical concedes the thing.

For it feels as though the bulls-eye and its aft-missed
　　outer ring
Has exchanged places with twenty radials,
And the poor artillery sling sees the shambling,
　　shuffling masses
And begins its booming swing.

And these penguins wobble toward the maws of the
    killer whale –
Seal complex and they gossip to one another as they
    wobble
To their deaths.
'Wouldn't this be perfect for wide-sweeping arcs of
    machine-gun
Fire,' they say above the din of wide-swept machine-
    gun fire,
'And these soaking sunken pot-holes here, what a
    sterling, hindering mire.'

And caught in a horizontal hail storm with leaking
    umbrellas –
All fine, stoic fellas – and long without a hat,
Not one bothered ask in any too-late moan
That perhaps they might have stayed away, in the
    trench
Or back at home, or in any other place for that cosy
    matter.

And shuffling forward, gentlemen to the last,
'Ladies first' someone jests and lets a lioness past.

And no queue-moaning was at all evinced,
As they watched for that vanguard clod of hooves,
And those long lines of paw prints.

Jutland, 31 May – 1 June

The last and largest of the great battleship bust-ups,
Both sides petrified, conscious of winter on the cusp
   of June,
Of not 'losing the war in an afternoon.'

Bulging fleets; frantic over the value of the
   Leviathans they'd bought,
Both sides terrified about the other side's
   dreadnoughts.

Both sides simply desperate not to lose,
Determined not to sail back with the wrong damned
   news.

So Jellicoe is no Nelson
And Jutland is no Trafalgar.
And heavyweights bouts are sometimes tame
And cannot hold our nostalgia.

The Lull

Today a lull.
Tonight most like a fight.
Bubbling antebellum for
England's thank-you polites.
Right now, nothing.
Save water in the boots.

But, tomorrow.
Now there lies a riddle.
For tomorrow they are saying
We're leaving this puddle,
This grotesque sleeping bag of men
And worms and lice. Of men and
Germs and mice.

And everything I had only seen
In the countryside as specimens
Of a vulgar and vile life.

We shall scram from this place.
We shall rise from this putrid
Medieval disgrace.
We shall slide across this sludge-glen.
And we shall rise, we are told, as men.

For tomorrow, we, the smite-brigade,
Are to have a walking race. To-morrow
We shall grace No Man's Land
With an attempted coup.

Though Whose Man's Land it will be
The day after tomorrow is understood
By few.
Most likely it will still be unclaimed –
Chartered, but in vain.

And most likely I will die.

Then let it be known
I tried to preserve some dignity.
I tried, I try, in this here foul mud pie.

The Attic

'Not that one.'
'Oh come on, it's junk. It's the kind of thing people keep because they're addicted to false nostalgia. Scared of change. Toss it, Bernard.'

So Bernard tossed it with the rest and listened to the clunk it made in the cardboard box where it came to rest.

'Not that one'
'Oh come on, Bernard. It's worthless. It's less than zero to you. Why are you so precious about all this crap you accrue? You're like dust itself sometimes, just happy to sprawl wherever. Toss it in the to-go box, it's not a bloody treasure.'

'Not that one.'

Mary held it aloft and inspected it anew. She threw it with the others but Bernard sprinted and ransacked the box, plucked it out and wiped his forehead with an almighty phew.

'Not this one,' he said. 'By Christ I'd forgot I had it, not this one ever, and My God I forgot I'd had it, not this one Mary for every kiss in the world, and this one won't be chucked out, for it truly is a pearl.'

'Well, what is it?' she said, alive with interest pricked. 'Is it gold? It looks a bit like gold lipstick.'

'It's a bullet, Mary, from two old grand-dads back. It's a shell from the war, it was the one that hit his calf – you know, I thought this was in my special drawer.'

'Well I haven't touched your special drawer, Bernie'

'Well someone must have moved it, and to think had I been down there making a cuppa whilst you were here purging me of my things, it would be gone. The bullet would be gone. To where would it go? This blood bullet, Mary? Hmmm? Well now I'm gonna clean it and watch it fucking glow.'

'You're crying,' she said. 'I'm sorry, Bernie I really am, it's been years since I saw you weep.'

'It's just the kind of thing, love, you really are meant to keep. It was given unto me by dad and given in good faith – it's the kind of thing I'm meant to keep quite genuinely safe.'

'From the First War?' she said as he descended the attic steps.

'Yep,' he said. 'From the war. The first I suppose you should say, though I remember it was still the war whenever granddad told it – *the war*,' he said and Mary heard him turn the key of his special treasures drawer.

Verdun Veteran

He is away now, just across the tableaux –
Away from the Rosbifs with their Dimanche
Wreaths of Brussels Sprouts and Potato bouts –
Until he sees something about this plate, and he
Springs from his low.

Once done with his remembering he sits up straight.
His back is there but not his head; his head
Isn't in it at all, and he dribbles on the mint sauce –
    on the beef, not his chin –
And he'll tuck into it and we'll begin in good posture
    and for just a second, he'll be back,
Away from the noise and glaze-winter of his eyes
    and all that.
And looking around the room – whether
For a bayonet or a broom –
He'll study us and smile
Like he knows he's been away,
Like time was ever present,
And he'll come back for that second, back into the
    real;
A little sad, maybe, but still seemingly wanting to
    heal.

But for each second-spark of better-now with him
   being back
It's fifty nine of pain; of strife, suffer, stretch and
   strain.
The clock is one sixtieth good for us, though it's
   majority bad,
We just need to learn the knack of being fifty-nine
   parts sad.

❦

Conscientious Objector

Man of peace during call of war,
What are your protestations for?
Are you above this? Is that what it is?
Do you see the world as being essentially warm?
And will you object to the Kaiser, refuse to perform,
When he arrives on these shores with his friends
In full swarm?

Man who says no, how's goes the road
And will you play truant at home?
Will you go cavorting, whoring,
Whisky drinking, whilst you're all alone?
In protest's forlorn company, with a wartime
Traitor's yawn.

Join the lasses in the factory? And when they ask,
Shouldn't you be in a trench? You'll
Say, 'Moi, non, je deteste les French.'

Conscientious objector. Who do you think you are?
Pacifist. Coward. Idiot. Nobody wants to spar;
It's a case, you see,
Of duty and its star.

Reputations

That reputations rest on racks of memory tests,
That Christmas Truces shine bright, still-blessed.
And you know in jubilation at the commencement of
   peace
They carried the 'Butcher' Haig through the jubilant
   streets.

Dorothy Lawrence

Bypassing the 'temporary men' at home,
Working the land or suspended on
Munitionette strands,
She clicked her heels three times
And ended up at the Front –
AKA Denis Smith –
Careful not to giggle,
Careful just to grunt.

So Dorothy, a lady through
And through, In Cognito and
In a uniform with a view,
Strapped down the hourglass
And cotton-bulked the shoulders,
And ever canary chirped
And every boulder smouldered.

And so she became a Tunneller
Of all the damned vocations.

And asked, in this grunt-giggling
At her cold, doleful station
Why her voice was not the hollower –
She was discovered, unveiled, presumed
A lewd 'camp follower.'

They meant whore.
Was she a lady of the night who
Tunnelled for men's money
And made their boredom rise
Like kites?

Flora Sandes

The only fairer to be a front-line bearer
Yorkshire born, Serbia bred, thinner in the arm,
Madder in the head.
And the heart.
And she poured forth
From emergency to emergency.
From place to place.
Who was she?
And what was her ploy?
This mischievous and brave,
Little free tomboy.

Her back was scraped and scrubbed
Roughly by a bomb.
In hand-to-hand fighting
She found her valour's beauty balm.

A childhood of horse riding and shooting,
And wishing for boy's warfare,
Whilst reciting Tennyson at full-throttle
In Suffolk's apple lairs.

Horrendous at housekeeping,
Overfond of booze and fags –
The fauna of the Balkans,
Just one of the lads.

Proud of being a woman,
But prouder still of babes who spar.
A 'Sworn virgin', if you can believe her version,
Now go show her where the
Wild things are.

Maria Bochkareva

The war for you was liberation;
Civilization.
From the cold of Siberia and the men who
Beat you into hurried hysteria.

War can give meaning
To those peace-pining demeanings of home
With its blizzards of humdrum brutality.

War years for you were the sweetened
Digresses and so on the platform you implored
Your woman folk to war, to fight, 'to become tigresses.'
And you hounded Kerensky to form a battalion
Of your own;

Bring out the women, let them do their press-ups
Shoot down nasty Germans, you'll them how to set up.
Bring out the women, you said, put the men to shame.
Let them drop dumbstruck, agape with fog-cloud
Vodka breath at the ballsy, at the brassy,
Bochkarevian Battallion of Death.

Confession of a Once Would-be Pastor

I used to be more religious.
Used to truly believe.
War has changed all that.
It's made me more man-conceive.
For in this world may lay the doom.
In this earth our only tomb.

With these new guns and these gas attacks,
One must ask what hell will be like.
What in store it has invented.
Fire-pikes?
For I've seen flame-throwers enfilade

My brothers in the trenches.
Ice then, perhaps?
For I've heard they froze at Caporetto,
Fortissimo to the last.

After our deaths and blackness falls
Does paradise yield or just Flanders Field?

Come now, tell me if you know, you
Brave war mongers who
Claim that empires must be laid,
That certain policies are sacrosanct,
That certain policies must be prayed.

That a man like the Archduke must be
Avenged whatever roughshod. Well then,

You have avenged the Archduke.
But you have killed God.

Ladder

Though I gripped the scale ladder and begged for palm-glue
The pal below cheered his "Boo-hoo'. It's the same for you,
   as for me,
That's why they call it camaraderie. You gonna stand there
   all day
As your pals slide down the pit? Stay below? Pretend you're
   hit?'

Mud

Only we know mud can smile.
Cough. Slurp. Spray. Burp.
It leaks on us like faeces.
It trickles us berserk.

Only we know mud can slide
Like ancient painter's envy.
Mud's patterns flow upon us –
Mud is slave. Mud is free.

Only we know mud can speak.
Squawk. Squish. Slobber. Splatter.
An orchestra of sloshes,
Mud is all which matters

Only we know mud can cackle.
Cocoon. Caress. Cloak. Chomp.
Sleeping in its blanket,
Waking in its romp.

Only we know mud rules
Like mermaids know the surf.
We know we're mud's fools
Mud in death. Mud in serf.

No-Mud's-Land does not exist
And we should know the better
Only Mud can win the war
For the drier or the wetter.

I wonder if this is a high point?

I wonder if this is a high point or whether there's
   more to come.
Some kind of conclusion to a century come undone?

Future forces yet to glean for future scholars to
   show?
For aspiring annalists and learned panelists with
   library books in tow?
For German apologists or archaeologists whose
   spades begin to glow?

Unearthing some structural puppetry, striking some
   extant subtlety,
Something clever, something we soldiers cannot
   know?

Or was it all just an anomaly? Some hoodwinked-
   hoaxed homily?
Or was the Devil actually the Kaiser? Will
   revisionism be so much wiser?

Silence superstitious soldier who knows the better
    than that.
Don't you know we sun-revolve and how the Earth
    isn't one bit flat?

But I wonder if this is a high point or it's only just
    begun.
Some inconclusive fore to a century still to come.

Shell-shock

The world's sweetest euphemism
For perhaps its crudest blow.

Shell-shock. War neurosis. Combat stress.
'Not quite himself' – that's what went to press.

Bayoneting the faces of snarling foes. Bound
To keep a man nervy, dancing on his toes.

Breaking out into an endless blubber. Thousand
Yard staring your once-close lover. She asks 'What's

Wrong?' You say 'Something is on my nerves,
That's all. Something's got on my nerves.'

'But what?' she asks. 'Come now, you're home
And you're big and tough and oh-so-strong.'

Chiming of the Waking

They sprang and sprawled and spread across the skies
Bone-starlings in rag-tag uniforms, half-bleeding, some gas-
    masked,
Stoned or drunk with glee and honour;

'Remember us,' they sang 'For we are all now long-goners,
Taken in our prime. And please not just those little myth-bits
    and folklores,
Those old mottos and maxims which handily rhyme.

Or you condemn us, you see,' they said as they chased each
    other with glee
'You belittle us. You demean us. You reduce us by degrees.
For we are more than little date-chimes' they said. 'Or
    memory-jogged classroom lines,
Confused rememberings of half-hearted accuracy,
Little tidbits in the fog of something that makes
You feel slightly guilty and small.'

And here they performed some manoeuvre in the skies and
    dropped in an open freefall.

'It's only you,' they said as they freely fell, 'who can preserve
    these fields. You,
As the undertakers of our tombs.
So don't get too caught up in timely, treasured dates but
    commemorate us late and soon.
And search for a legacy in the trivial, from the mustard on
    your chips
To the gas attack in the classroom when someone's egg has
    slipped.'

The starling formation of soldier-ghosts swooned down
Amongst the Forget-Me-Nots
And plopped to earth and formed a tank, a-roared with their
    howitzer snouts and
Trundled into the Belgian forest – Wheat beers and wheat-
    beer louts.

And now a mine blew that tank apart into a million ghost
    atoms
And they blew back into their tombs as dusk shell-burst its
    somber pattern.

A lonesome cross levitated above the fallow field;
A soldier, crucified, revealed – tied upon a clock's
    determined hands
Floating into legacy upon this barren land.

'Remember us all,' the soldier chimed and shot off into
    heaven,
Gleeful and leaven in his juvenescent prime.

So back they went, these soldier-ghosts, back to the shrieked
    and golden light.
Back to mind the dawn. Back to mind the night.

Voles

Dearest Elspeth,
We are armies of voles munching
Through the continent. Perhaps we'll
Dig all the way to the Tsar's palace,
And create a new rail network.

It's astonishing, really.
'All aboard the Verdun-Vladivostok
The longest interconnected line
Of continuous trek-murk!'

Though, it's nothing like our bed at
Home, nothing like making love to you.
I still dream of that night hen and your
Whiteness at the kirk.

We have these odd things to do like
Morning to and stand hate. These odd
Rituals seem to frame our day's long,
Protracted wait.

Anyway, off to do the trench cycle
With love and lust
Your 'McRomeo' Michael
xxx

Splendid Isolation

They helped us out good, you have to admit. I don't think
   we'd have if they'd been fighting
The Canadians or the Mexicans or what have you. It was
   good of them to come; all roaring
And high-spirited − a little loud, a little too optimistic, but
   welcome for it and very good fun.

And now they want nothing of us.

They came over, all democratic and dogmatic − they even
   gave us the League − but they're
Gonna stay well clear; it's a present just for us, they're too
   busy, they say, with their war
Fatigue-liars! They weren't even in the war for long!
No, instead they have immigrants to check on, blacks to
   hang, evolution studies to dispel;
Reds to scare. Seems they've had enough of Europe and
   nothing will compel them to the
Old World with its old troublesome lairs.

And now they want nothing of us.

They have jazz to dance, flappers to kiss, cars to drive, roads
    to build, credit to pay for it too.
They have moonshine to sup, they have movie stars and
    gangsters and great big cities for
Any old rogue or chancer.

And now they want nothing of us.
And I don't blame them one bit.

Delville Wood

We rounded up the Boers after burning them from farm and
village.
We brought in the century with a new form of rape and
pillage.
And we, a little or a lot like Hitler would, had our relapse in
concentration camps –
Women and children only mind, Boer men were still out in
their battling ranks.

The 'Hell Camps' we gave them, halving rations as babies
died on the teets of Mothers,
Mothers pallored-ashen with the death upon them –
cramped, crabbed and smothered.
In Bloemfontein just thirteen toilets for a whole camp to
flush their leans
And did twenty-two thousand children have to perish, all
under sixteen?

But they stood in the way of Britain and the Transvaal Gold
   and so we herded
Them like cattle, herded them into simple camps of blood.
Herded, perhaps, because at the time, herd we could.
But things can change, things can unfold. For all of this; they
   came. They came. All told.
Smuts and Botha and the troops did us good, and their
   corpses
And their memories are camped in Delville Wood.

Stiff Upper Englishness

Our uniform has something of sartorial splendour about it –
Dashing coiffure of ammunition stitches,
Mills bombs in a chic bandolier,
Shovels and webbings too – despite the fact we don't get
    near.

We walk, empire-talk,
Toward the wired mizzen-mist
On this, our symbolic little death spree,
And in our grand gesture towards war, Sergeant Clarke
Said, 'We're a little like the Matebele, whooping toward
The maxim guns.'

Though we don't whoop. We mostly chatter idly
About nothing much but life and its ways. Like,
'Excuse me, friend, won't you pass the Earl Gris?
Oh, you're Dead. Well, as I say, excuse me.'

We keep up appearances, our
Spirits are still pure.

The Unknown Soldier

The. Not *A*, or more properly *An*,
The soldier, probably young; probably a man.
Much more than that we don't really know
'cept he died in the try, in the sun or the snow.

Yet *An* Unknown Soldier amends somewhat –
Makes the missing more molten in war's running plot.
Somehow more personal, like a you or a me,
Makes him somehow more lost to cold futility.

And too, it changes the sense. And too, it changes the scent.
It really does. It alters what was, what *is*, meant.
An Unknown Soldier; now what does that say
Indeed? What does *An* Unknown Soldier say
About Anonymity?

An hints at a name we are not to know.
An presumes an identity, a fellow with
Foibles and troubles, with a future still yet to grow.

But it's *The*. The article is *the*. It's all those *Ans*
Aggregated into this single one. All that neutrality
Honoured, or simplified; one for all. All or none.

This notion of an Unknown fighting thing
Stretching out to all Unknown fighting things
And in this great stretching of herdsmanship
It brings all the lost warriors under some candle
Of fellowship.

Death in the Trenches

The cruellest slice is random death.
The Reaper's sword. His vile breath.
A random shell.
You have no real influence where it fell.
If you're busy cleaning weapon,
Or catching a few quick snores.
Where it falls it falls and where it falls it scores.

Then comes disease.
Sickle swooshed sneeze and sprays those whom it hates,
Those whom it loves,
Those it only likes,
Whomever it please.
Even the rats can smell the fungus and are as sickly as to
    chase the cats,
And the men chase the hens as France becomes the Fens.

You can also freeze.
When the water's at your knees, and the sickle comes
    pouring
And shivers in the reeves.
And being cold, so cold and wet
You need a fucking vet,
Is most bad for a poor man's soul.
It's the enemy and the enemy's enemy. It's where he
    doubles his blows.

And collapse.
Collapse is cruel like evaporated gruel.
This fate I avoided yesterday; he had his eyes on me and
    so too his shells.
The wall caved in but I was rescued – thank God, I was
    rescued well.
The wall caved in but I laughed where it fell,
At the arrow of time and the ringing of the bell
And how the grain blew strong
Despite this shark of a sickle,
And how the crop refused to harvest and how the Reaper
    was so fickle.

Gangrene. Septicemia. Trench Fever, Exposure,
　Boredom. Lice.
Mice. Frogs. Dreams of sermons.
Most Germans.
And dreams of Mary Pickford. Or rotten duckboard. Or
　if you're dick-bored
And you have Pickford in her ermine
And old Complacency slices what you should already
　have as Learning.

Anyone of them could do. Anyone could be
Death punishment number 1.
My only hope, little brother, so that again I may see you,
Is for something like trench foot or very sick leave or
　serious injury –
His 'see you soon sucker,' death punishment number 2.

All Hail the Trench

Ingenious warrens of safety,
Who knows how many lives
Saved, cocooned, incubated in
Its magnificent mazety.

Democratic rotations, even when
They Flood – each man takes his
Turn in this fate-flung mud.

These tunnels are our castles,
Our pride, our capsized marquees,
And we Englishmen are vassals
To every French marquis.

Thousands of kilometres they go and go.
All dug by men too, each indent in the earth
The result of our toil.
It's an extraordinary feat,
Bodes well for future roil!

Eastern Front

You recall with timidity
Our battles blazing in fluidity –
Movement, motion, mistake –
The Somme, Verdun, Marne, Champagne –
Pah!
Mere static battles of breakthrough and brake.

And what of Tannenberg? What of the Masurian Lakes?

Habsburgs, Ottomans, Tsardoms – such were the players,
Such were the stakes.
We went hammer and tongues through the fires of summer,
Through endless blizzards of flakes.

But Wild East and Muddy West,
It is the mud-slumps which have been preserved the best.
A country remembers its own wars fine,
Those in other's spheres are a little more benign.

Medusa

We now see what our legendary artillery barrage has done.
Wonderful, effective thing. It has made the barbed wire
   more bird-nest like and – Wonderful, effective thing –
   impenetrable. The snakes are not impressed.
She is today an especially enraged, entangled Medusa, we've
   given her an earache
She refuses to come the looser to English secateurs or the
   most cordial non-sequiturs.

Atlee

Top Hat tails and little left wing sails
Which blew East to London's poor
Then further still,
Blew from one road to another;
One entirely paved uphill.

And so you signed up as your
Own brother said no,
For no isms, aims or ideas

Ever came about, you sensed,
Through wistful Ave Marias.
Never just through blind hope.

And you, in full clemency, found
Yourself with the South Lancs
In Gallipoli.
At best and at worst, you
Fell ill with dysentery.

Was this the death throes of the
Fairer state?
The man who would oust even
Winston
From the history books?

One in whom the Promised Land
Had promised so much;
Found its own head-strong, prince-son
Laid down with the bloody Flux.

It's not right, this left man must
Have thought
Convalescing in a Maltese hospital.
It is too unfair.
Though as you convalesced weren't your

Comrades killed in the
Battle of Sari Blair –
What had you been there?
Had you been spared?
Is it worth the thinking about houses and
Healthcare?

And here, at Gallipoli,
Your admiration for Churchill
Began in loan and
Bloomed into being his deputy during the
Wartime coalition. But, then,
What was left of the War was not right
And some cigars don't listen to the
Fumidor's endless trite.

And so, all roads must, too, assess Rome.
Acknowledge that what is great and linked
Abroad must be greater still
At Home.

And roads and myths of
Horses and raiders
And story's spun by cowards and bravers.
Attlee.
The Lawyer became soldier,
Became the caped crusader.

Sharks About

I have conferred widely along the trench line and we,
   Company B, have elected that the
War is run by Sharks. Swimming in the Kaiser Palace and
   swimming with the Tsar.
Swimming with old Georgie and drowning at the bar,
Their chosen teeth are shrapnel which they thrash from afar.

Versailles

Diktat; dictated peace – well perhaps
It was – and true they were weak.
But they never ended up paying,
A thing worth the saying
And though it was Harsh – as
Harsh as instant death to the newly-freed –
It was nothing to the way they would
Have gladly seen us bleed.

Harsh, was it, in retrospect –
The fact France was vindictive
With half its country wrecked.
Or that Britain towed a midline
Between revenge and peace,
And did it aid Britain,
This attempt of the meek?

Beautiful chateaux. Beautiful gardens.
Perhaps here once lied the chance
For History's pardon.

Two Flus

Man's flu united millions around the world in common
    cause.
Nature's flu didn't, it played by its own indiscernible laws.
You can die by a bullet or by the older ways still
For there is no war that can compete with being deadly ill.

Lessines

Did they tire at the gloating machines or scoff at the onset of
    peace
That soon for them would be plough-in-the-sky. Soon would
    be nought
But neighbours and off-to farmland goodbyes. And did they
    gallop and
Then canter and then trot? Bowed bridles flecked with tears,
    heads raised
With final banter. One last forage; one last breach

And did they run for freedom or the past, for the first of
    them or the last?
Did they sense their time had come, like glass-less eyes
    blinking
In the sun, and now had almost gone, like a long sabre's
    threat to a bomb.
And were there jokes-insiders; I bet there were, yays and
    neighs and talk of
Destiny's ways – and, then, what too of the riders?

For they set off just ten minutes before the end of the race, one
Last hurdle; one last chase. When the machine guns stopped at the
Stroke of eleven, did man and horse bray, call it a day, cross
Themselves to rest in rural heaven? And perhaps what was the
Point, the history books will oink, why would any man or boy or
Horse in Troy go to battle ten minutes before the end of the war?

But we didn't get to ask them why. Why they thundered down the
Cobbled streets and the bullets yawn-flew from the windows of the
Plagued Lessines. Glorified and emancipated through hooves and
Hearts with but one minute of war left to their art. 'Onwards to the bridge
At Dendre' they cried, gallop quick. And, in fact, it was gallop-saved from its
Last second demolition-tick.

Thrust, Twist

Such a simple instruction. Thrust and Twist.
Like a dance move. 'Send it home,' they used to say.
Send it home. Make it count. Tears for you if you missed.
Get close enough. Stab 'em. Make 'em pay.

Basra, 1914-2014

The Anglo-Persian Oil Company knows what it's about.
Like the East India before, it trades and trades with clout.
Empire-building if it must and on lookout for trading spoils
Britain has its coal, you see, but it doesn't have much oil.

So it was oil for the first time, liberation the second.
Where once we could so beckon so now we are beckoned.
Where once we mobilised the world as we pawn-push-
    pleased,
So we are now mobilised for a larger Empire's needs.

Pulse

The Seas in desperation, the tide unsure which way to turn
The British navy on globe-patrol; portside, starboard, bow
    and stern.
China, Africa, Liberia, Fiji, Japan, Brazil, India, Trinidad –
Even troops under Kilimanjaro's shadow – the world was
    pulsing mad.

From around the world they came by their destituted dozens,
For a white man's war. For Anglo-Saxon-Slavic cousins.
They fought for mother countries despite the maternal abuse
Outposts without votes died for Poseidon, Hades and Zeus.

Kiev to Kingston; Melbourne to Montreal. Sarajevo to
    Sofia.
Bulawayo to Berlin and back again, war pulsed in every
    sphere.

India

As soon as Britain embroils itself in war, India
In her heathen, polytreacherous ways, will
Strike for independence, mark these words
While we fight half-Christians, she'll become the Hindia.

Yet India rallied. Pallied. Tallied over a million,
Half-bankrupted herself in her role as pillion and
Fought in every theatre of war, killing fellow Muslims,
Freezing at Ypres; storming for us throughout the Middle
    East.

The largest voluntary force in history, the rubies of the
Jewel in the crown. They hoped-for independence, after
This sacrificial spritzer; but those hopes drowned and
    glugged
And Thames-tonic judged. We stirred only a vile Amritsar.

And the old colonial lie and the old colonies always die
And it takes blood not loyalty to be free, or non-violence,
If that be the spread of the ghee, but almost never is it
Dulce et decorum est pro patria mater mori.

LBW

Leg Before Wicket. Life Before Wife.
Strong Yorkshire. Strong England.
Same at Headingley as Passchendaele really.

I was co-opted to throw the
Pineapples, as the most accurate
In my regiment. Must hurl a Mills
Overarm – I used to spin them slightly,
Not to turn it legside, just to keep me sprightly.

The Bombs

My God. At the beginning, the jam tin bombs.
Crashed like a concerto of badly blared Brahms.
Lit by Cigarettes they were. And stuffed under corpses
Or otherwise the innards of doomed dead horses.

Empire

And the day before Christmas the turkey feels full, never
   brimmed so big with the feed in it,
Never had such a feast as to the day preceding its cull.

Tanganyiki, Syria, Jordon, Palestine and Cameroon – it must
   have looked quite the boon
As the red map was redder and from an unthinkable war
   we'd done the unthinkable again;
The British Empire was even ruddy bigger. The Empire on
   which the sun never set had new
Places to bronze, to fan, to fuss, to sweat.

From Singapore to Cairo, from the Suez to the Cape, the
   banquet of the Atlas was ours –
Every spice on every plate.
And never had the silver spoon rebounded with such
   glimmer –
Yet it was high noon for us. British boils were on the simmer.

Common cause and commonwealth can do a lot to change
an Empire's health.
'And more red maybe your flapping wings,' to stout
Britannia the stouter Lady sings.
'But it's high noon for you,' she crooned, 'now count the
evening's cost of war.'
And all those Yanks in thanks, their dollars flickering, asking
if she knew any more?

Salonika 1

Did Olympus do a double-take at the swarms of men and
    the hives they make?
As alliance wars stirred below between old friends and new
    felons.
As morning's butterfly makes midday's bellum.

Sparta and its friends
Versus Athens and its friends in Peloponnesian hysteria.

Now revived by peacetime pacts of British, French, Russians,
Serbs and Greeks, split in civil pique
Against Germans, Austrians, Hungarians –
Now joined by late Bulgaria.

For alliances are eternal and the pacts of man diurnal –
Nor do they ever end.
Nor does war ever let off what in peace it lends
And nor do mountains or malaria.

Salonika 2

Polyglot forces in wretched Muckydonia.
Sweating in trenches of Olives.
Denied home leave; reviled local leave,
Pipped in memory by other soldiers in better theatres with
better theatre-payers.

Bored in a remote part of antiquity where planes strafed
men and men strafed prayers.
Freezing in the nights from the cruel Vardar winds,
In daytime sweating ichor;
Mocked with the moniker of 'The Gardeners of Salonika'

But all men's fate lies were they are sent and you cultivated
Greece with
The service you rent. And as the Bulgarians crumbled,
And the Front broke forth, just days before you forced the
end of war,
Did the Gods watch the Kaiser jump
Into the Rhine when his soldiers came back with a Black
Flag at the wrong place
And the wrong time.

Coward

Vile and sick and cowardly and more, to not go where the
  wind blows,
To pull the sheets over the head, to ignore the banging door.
To be some disgrace. To not go where the wind blows.
And who can defy the wind, which leaf can take leave of the
  way the trees bow,
Which man can say no?
All men must go.

And what do you think life is, some blank slate
Or blanker cheque? A paradise?
That you embody nature's intended state.

That you were born into the universe.
That you did not grow out of it, grow from it,
But were forced into its scandalous conspiracy.

Well the wind does blows and cannot complain of its endless
  breeze.
How can you not read war into the story of man? What do
  you think of lions and dinosaurs and pacifistic cavemen?
To hell with you, coward.

The Christmas Centenary Truce

The first goal fettered out
And we were embarrassed by their riches,
Their gross wages, their era, their luck.

They almost celebrated
But didn't, couldn't, thought better of it;
Repressed the desire of the schoolyard boast.

They won. In a sense.
And, in obligatory sportsmanship,
Despite the victory it went to pens.

Pens against the Germans!
They saluted. Shook hands. And the chastened
Commentators fell quiet, almost sullen,

Almost rattled,
When the montage of the trenches broadcast
On stadia screens. Some players and pundits would

Much preferred to have
Stayed well indoors, spending Christmas at home,
That, trust them, unlucky ones. Put upon,

Noblesse Oblige.
To have to spend Christmas day in effing snowy
Belgium. Thank God they weren't in uniform–

Suggested by some
Left-wing loons at the Beeb. Bloody nutters.
For Christmas is a rare and sacred time. All

Decent, Godly folk
Should spend it with family and friends. And
Who gives a shit about a stupid old

Centenary. Huh?
Why bother, it means nothing to us now.
But millions watched it all the same. At home,

In High Yuletide,
Laughing at our premiership players
And the things famous people have to do.

8995876R00077

Printed in Great Britain
by Amazon.co.uk, Ltd.,
Marston Gate.